OUR GRATITUDE JOURNAL

52 WEEKS OF LOVE, MINDFULNESS, AND APPRECIATION FOR COUPLES

MARCUS AND ASHLEY KUSI

Our Gratitude Journal: 52 Weeks of Love, Mindfulness, and Appreciation for Couples

ISBN-13: 978-1-949781-00-7

Introduction

"Gratitude is the golden frame through which we see the meaning of life."
–Brendon Burchard

Expressing gratitude is a unique way to show you love, value, and appreciate your partner. Something different occurs when you write down or express the thoughts of gratitude you have for your partner. By writing down your gratitude, you can easily share your thoughts with your partner and even read them over and over again as loving reminders throughout your years together.

That's why we created *Our Gratitude Journal*, a weekly journal for you and your partner to write in and show how much you appreciate each other. It's a weekly activity you can do together, to increase happiness, reduce stress, and strengthen your relationship. More importantly, you will be focusing on the positives of your partner, and nurturing a grateful attitude.

By truly reflecting on all the wonderful ways your partner supports you each week, you will have more empathy for your partner, feel appreciated, and see how important you are to each other. Also, it will connect you and your partner on a deeper level, reducing the number of conflicts you have.

That being said, gratitude journaling is an easy and simple way to practice mindfulness. Journaling how grateful you are for each other will make you more aware of the good things your partner does and the wonderful things about them.

Now, use *Our Gratitude Journal* to record and keep track of all the wonderful things that you are grateful for your partner each week. So you can improve your relationship, strengthen your intimacy and your love for each other.

> "Gratitude is the healthiest of all human emotions. The more you express gratitude for what you have, the more likely you will have even more to express gratitude for."
> –Zig Ziglar

How to Use This Journal

"An attitude of gratitude brings great things."
– Yogi Bhajan

First, at the end of each week, think about at least one genuine thing you are grateful for about your partner, or something they did during the week that you appreciate. It can be something you learned from your partner. It can be something inspiring, silly, or a funny joke your partner said that made your day or week. The next section has gratitude prompts you can refer to.

Second, for consistency, schedule time to complete your section for the week. You can do it together or separately. Then choose a deadline you both should complete your respective sections by. A deadline will ensure you do not postpone that week's journaling and let it run into the next week.

Make your weekly journaling experience even better by reading and discussing what you journal each week. A fun challenge is to complete this journal as a 52-week gratitude challenge.

Third, after completing your 52nd journal entries, complete the *52 Week Journal Reflections* exercise. Then share with each other the top 3 journal entries from your partner that you loved the most. Tell your partner why you loved each gratitude entry.

Lastly, always remember to include *why* you are grateful for your partner when you complete your gratitude entry for the week.

Gratitude Journaling Prompts for Couples

Use the prompts below to make your weekly journaling easier.

What is something your partner did during the week that:

1. You are thankful or grateful for.

Listened to your excitements or frustrations.

Were patient when you would have lost it.

Supported and encouraged your decision(s).

Cared for you due to sickness.

Made you feel safe to be emotionally vulnerable.

Asked for your opinion on something.

Cooked a meal or packed lunch for you.

Gave you a nice back, head, neck, shoulder, or full body massage.

Had a deep conversation about your relationship, or opened up to you.

2. Made you feel appreciated.

A compromise.

A difficult conversation that improved your relationship.

Something he/she did but would not normally do (like an activity you love but your partner may not).

Was honest and sincere even when it hurt.

Gave you alone time.

Remembered something important for you.

Did something you forgot to do (like a chore).

Apologized to you.

3. Made you feel loved.

A passionate hug.

The amazing and satisfying sex you had.

Achieved a bucket list goal with you.

Exercised with you.

Thanked you for the little and big things.

Complimented you.

Called or texted just to see how you are doing.

Sent you something that shows he/she was thinking of you.

4. You were happily surprised by.

A good morning note.

A sexy text message.

An unexpected gift (like flowers).

Waking up to a very clean house.

5. You truly enjoyed.

Something they did for no reason.

A parenting moment that you were awed by.

A love letter.

A family event you attended.

Another event you attended together.

An engaging and fun conversation you had.

6. Made you feel special or smile.

Praised you in front of other people.

Cherished something you did for him/her.

Stood up for you.

7. You learned from.

A new skill.

A quicker way to do something.

His/her optimism.

A mindset shift.

Discovered something about yourself.

Let go of a fear.

Dealt with emotions, stress, insecurities, etc.

8. Made things easier for you.

Helped with home life, household chores, and/or errands.

Purchased something that added value to your lives.

Got rid of something you dislike.

Noticed when you were overwhelmed, tired or exhausted, and did something to help you feel better.

9. You want to recognize.

Graduated from school.

Got a job promotion or pay raise.

Volunteered his/her time and/or money.

1

This Week _____

_____

_____

_____

_____

_____

_____

_____

_____

_____

_____

Date _____

"As we express our gratitude, we must never forget that the highest appreciation is not to utter words, but to live by them."
-John F. Kennedy

This Week _____

_____

_____

_____

_____

_____

_____

_____

_____

_____

_____

Date _____

2

This Week _____

_____

_____

_____

_____

_____

_____

_____

_____

_____

_____

Date _____

*"The deepest principle in human nature
is the craving to be appreciated."*
–William James

This Week _____

_____

_____

_____

_____

_____

_____

_____

_____

_____

_____

Date _____

3

This Week _____

_____

_____

_____

_____

_____

_____

_____

_____

_____

_____

Date _____

"Those with a grateful mindset tend to see the message in the mess. And even though life may knock them down, the grateful find reasons, if even small ones, to get up." –Steve Maraboli

This Week _____

_____

_____

_____

_____

_____

_____

_____

_____

_____

_____

Date _____

4

This Week _____

_____

_____

_____

_____

_____

_____

_____

_____

_____

_____

Date _____

"Treat people as if they were what they ought to be and you help them to become what they are capable of being."
-Johann Wolfgang von Goethe

This Week _____

_____

_____

_____

_____

_____

_____

_____

_____

_____

_____

Date _____

5

This Week _____

_____

_____

_____

_____

_____

_____

_____

_____

_____

_____

Date _____

"Love is made up of three unconditional properties in equal measure: acceptance, understanding, and appreciation. Remove any one of the three and the triangle falls apart." –Vera Nazarian

This Week _____

_____

_____

_____

_____

_____

_____

_____

_____

_____

_____

Date _____

6

This Week _____

_____

_____

_____

_____

_____

_____

_____

_____

_____

_____

_____

Date _____

"I love you, not only for what you are, but for what I am when I am with you. I love you, not only for what you have made of yourself, but for what you are making of me." –Roy Croft

This Week _____

_____

_____

_____

_____

_____

_____

_____

_____

_____

_____

Date _____

7

This Week _____

_____

_____

_____

_____

_____

_____

_____

_____

_____

_____

Date _____

"To find someone who will love you for no reason, and to shower that person with reasons, that is the ultimate happiness."
–Robert Brault

This Week _____

_____

_____

_____

_____

_____

_____

_____

_____

_____

_____

Date _____

8

This Week _____

_____

_____

_____

_____

_____

_____

_____

_____

_____

_____

Date _____

"You will find, as you look back upon your life, that the moments when you have truly lived are the moments when you have done things in the spirit of love." –Henry Drummond

This Week _____

_____

_____

_____

_____

_____

_____

_____

_____

_____

_____

Date _____

9

This Week _____

_____

_____

_____

_____

_____

_____

_____

_____

_____

_____

_____

Date _____

"The more you practice gratitude, the more you see how much there is to be grateful for, and your life becomes an ongoing celebration of joy and happiness." –Don Miguel Ruiz

This Week _____

_____

_____

_____

_____

_____

_____

_____

_____

_____

_____

Date _____

10

This Week _____

_____

_____

_____

_____

_____

_____

_____

_____

_____

_____

Date _____

"A word of encouragement from a spouse can save a marriage."
–John C. Maxwell

This Week _____

_____

_____

_____

_____

_____

_____

_____

_____

_____

_____

Date _____

11

This Week _____

_____

_____

_____

_____

_____

_____

_____

_____

_____

_____

_____

Date _____

"To be fully seen by somebody, then, and be loved anyhow-this is a human offering that can border on miraculous." –Elizabeth Gilbert

This Week _____

_____

_____

_____

_____

_____

_____

_____

_____

_____

_____

Date _____

12

This Week _____

_____

_____

_____

_____

_____

_____

_____

_____

_____

_____

_____

Date _____

"Love is a partnership of two unique people who bring out the very best in each other, and who know that even though they are wonderful as individuals, they are even better together."
–Barbara Cage

This Week _____

_____

_____

_____

_____

_____

_____

_____

_____

_____

_____

Date _____

13

This Week _____

_____

_____

_____

_____

_____

_____

_____

_____

_____

_____

Date _____

"Thank you is the best prayer that anyone could say. I say that one a lot. Thank you expresses extreme gratitude, humility, understanding." –Alice Walker

This Week _____

_____

_____

_____

_____

_____

_____

_____

_____

_____

_____

Date _____

14

This Week _____

_____

_____

_____

_____

_____

_____

_____

_____

_____

_____

_____

Date _____

"When we give cheerfully and accept gratefully, everyone is blessed." -Maya Angelou

This Week _____

_____

_____

_____

_____

_____

_____

_____

_____

_____

_____

Date _____

15

This Week _____

_____

_____

_____

_____

_____

_____

_____

_____

_____

_____

Date _____

"Feeling gratitude and not expressing it is like wrapping a present and not giving it." –**William Arthur Ward**

This Week _____

_____

_____

_____

_____

_____

_____

_____

_____

_____

_____

Date _____

16

This Week _____

_____

_____

_____

_____

_____

_____

_____

_____

_____

_____

Date _____

"Enjoy the little things, for one day you may look back and realize they were the big things." –Robert Brault

This Week _____

_____

_____

_____

_____

_____

_____

_____

_____

_____

_____

Date _____

17

This Week _____

_____

_____

_____

_____

_____

_____

_____

_____

_____

_____

Date _____

"The smallest act of kindness is worth more than the grandest intention." –Oscar Wilde

This Week _____

_____

_____

_____

_____

_____

_____

_____

_____

_____

_____

_____

Date _____

18

This Week _____

_____

_____

_____

_____

_____

_____

_____

_____

_____

_____

Date _____

"No one who achieves success does so without the help of others. The wise and confident acknowledge this help with gratitude."
—Alfred North Whitehead

This Week _____

_____

_____

_____

_____

_____

_____

_____

_____

_____

_____

Date _____

19

This Week _____

_____

_____

_____

_____

_____

_____

_____

_____

_____

_____

Date _____

"If you concentrate on finding whatever is good in every situation, you will discover that your life will suddenly be filled with gratitude, a feeling that nurtures the soul." –Rabbi Harold Kushner

This Week _____

_____

_____

_____

_____

_____

_____

_____

_____

_____

_____

_____

Date _____

20

This Week _____

_____

_____

_____

_____

_____

_____

_____

_____

_____

_____

Date _____

"Develop an attitude of gratitude, and give thanks for everything that happens to you, knowing that every step forward is a step toward achieving something bigger and better than your current situation." –Brian Tracy

This Week _____

_____

_____

_____

_____

_____

_____

_____

_____

_____

_____

Date _____

21

This Week _____

_____

_____

_____

_____

_____

_____

_____

_____

_____

_____

_____

Date _____

"Gratitude is the most exquisite form of courtesy."
–Jacques Maritain

This Week _____

_____

_____

_____

_____

_____

_____

_____

_____

_____

_____

Date _____

22

This Week _____

_____

_____

_____

_____

_____

_____

_____

_____

_____

_____

_____

Date _____

"Be grateful for what you have and stop complaining-it bores everybody else, does you no good, and doesn't solve any problems."
-Zig Ziglar

This Week _____

_____

_____

_____

_____

_____

_____

_____

_____

_____

_____

Date _____

23

This Week _____

_____

_____

_____

_____

_____

_____

_____

_____

_____

_____

Date _____

"I would maintain that thanks are the highest form of thought; and that gratitude is happiness doubled by wonder." –G.K. Chesterton

This Week _____

_____

_____

_____

_____

_____

_____

_____

_____

_____

_____

Date _____

24

This Week _____

_____

_____

_____

_____

_____

_____

_____

_____

_____

_____

_____

Date _____

"Acknowledging the good that you already have in your life is the foundation for all abundance." –Eckhart Tolle

This Week _____

_____

_____

_____

_____

_____

_____

_____

_____

_____

_____

Date _____

25

This Week _____

_____

_____

_____

_____

_____

_____

_____

_____

_____

_____

Date _____

"If a fellow isn't thankful for what he's got, he isn't likely to be thankful for what he's going to get." –Frank A. Clark

This Week _____

_____

_____

_____

_____

_____

_____

_____

_____

_____

_____

Date _____

26

This Week _____

_____

_____

_____

_____

_____

_____

_____

_____

_____

_____

_____

Date _____

"If you want to turn your life around, try thankfulness. It will change your life mightily." –Gerald Good

This Week _____

_____

_____

_____

_____

_____

_____

_____

_____

_____

_____

Date _____

27

This Week _____

_____

_____

_____

_____

_____

_____

_____

_____

_____

_____

Date _____

"Gratitude turns what we have into enough, and more.
It turns denial into acceptance, chaos into order, confusion
into clarity...it makes sense of our past, brings peace for today,
and creates a vision for tomorrow." – Melody Beattie

This Week _____

_____

_____

_____

_____

_____

_____

_____

_____

_____

_____

Date _____

28

This Week _____

_____

_____

_____

_____

_____

_____

_____

_____

_____

_____

_____

Date _____

"The way to develop the best that is in a person is by appreciation and encouragement." –Charles Schwab

This Week _____

_____

_____

_____

_____

_____

_____

_____

_____

_____

_____

Date _____

29

This Week _____

_____

_____

_____

_____

_____

_____

_____

_____

_____

_____

_____

Date _____

"He is a wise man who does not grieve for the things which he has not, but rejoices for those which he has." –Epictetus

This Week _____

_____

_____

_____

_____

_____

_____

_____

_____

_____

_____

Date _____

30

This Week _____

_____

_____

_____

_____

_____

_____

_____

_____

_____

_____

_____

Date _____

"The deepest craving of human nature is the need to be appreciated."
-**William James**

This Week _____

_____

_____

_____

_____

_____

_____

_____

_____

_____

_____

Date _____

31

This Week _____

_____

_____

_____

_____

_____

_____

_____

_____

_____

_____

_____

Date _____

"It is impossible to feel grateful and depressed in the same moment."
-Naomi Williams

This Week _____

_____

_____

_____

_____

_____

_____

_____

_____

_____

_____

Date _____

32

This Week _____

_____

_____

_____

_____

_____

_____

_____

_____

_____

_____

Date _____

"In ordinary life, we hardly realize that we receive a great deal more than we give, and that it is only with gratitude that life becomes rich." –Dietrich Bonhoeffer

This Week _____

_____

_____

_____

_____

_____

_____

_____

_____

_____

_____

Date _____

33

This Week _____

_____

_____

_____

_____

_____

_____

_____

_____

_____

_____

_____

Date _____

"Gratitude and attitude are not challenges; they are choices."
-Robert Braathe

This Week _____

_____

_____

_____

_____

_____

_____

_____

_____

_____

Date _____

34

This Week _____

_____

_____

_____

_____

_____

_____

_____

_____

_____

_____

Date _____

"Gratitude also opens your eyes to the limitless potential of the universe, while dissatisfaction closes your eyes to it."
–Stephen Richards

This Week _____

_____

_____

_____

_____

_____

_____

_____

_____

_____

_____

Date _____

35

This Week _____

_____

_____

_____

_____

_____

_____

_____

_____

_____

_____

Date _____

"Be thankful for what you have: you'll end up having more.
If you concentrate on what you don't have, you will
never, ever have enough." –Oprah Winfrey

This Week _____

_____

_____

_____

_____

_____

_____

_____

_____

_____

_____

Date _____

36

This Week _____

_____

_____

_____

_____

_____

_____

_____

_____

_____

_____

Date _____

"To get the full value of joy you must have someone to divide it with." –Mark Twain

This Week _____

_____

_____

_____

_____

_____

_____

_____

_____

_____

_____

Date _____

37

This Week _____

_____

_____

_____

_____

_____

_____

_____

_____

_____

_____

Date _____

"The invariable mark of wisdom is to see the miraculous in the common." –Ralph Waldo Emerson

This Week _____

_____

_____

_____

_____

_____

_____

_____

_____

_____

_____

Date _____

38

This Week _____

_____

_____

_____

_____

_____

_____

_____

_____

_____

_____

_____

Date _____

"Don't forget, a person's greatest emotional need is to feel appreciated." –H. Jackson Brown Jr.

This Week _____

_____

_____

_____

_____

_____

_____

_____

_____

_____

_____

Date _____

39

This Week _____

_____

_____

_____

_____

_____

_____

_____

_____

_____

_____

_____

Date _____

"I think for any relationship to be successful, there needs to be loving communication, appreciation, and understanding."
–Miranda Kerr

This Week _____

_____

_____

_____

_____

_____

_____

_____

_____

_____

_____

Date _____

40

This Week _____

_____

_____

_____

_____

_____

_____

_____

_____

_____

_____

_____

Date _____

"Find joy in everything you choose to do. Every job, relationship, home... it's your responsibility to love it, or change it."
–Chuck Palahniuk

This Week _____

_____

_____

_____

_____

_____

_____

_____

_____

_____

_____

Date _____

41

This Week _____

_____

_____

_____

_____

_____

_____

_____

_____

_____

_____

_____

Date _____

"They do not love that do not show their love."
–William Shakespeare

This Week _____

_____

_____

_____

_____

_____

_____

_____

_____

_____

Date _____

42

This Week _____

_____

_____

_____

_____

_____

_____

_____

_____

_____

_____

Date _____

"Feeling grateful or appreciative of someone or something in your life actually attracts more of the things that you appreciate and value into your life." –Northrup Christiane

This Week _____

_____

_____

_____

_____

_____

_____

_____

_____

_____

_____

Date _____

43

This Week _____

_____

_____

_____

_____

_____

_____

_____

_____

_____

_____

Date _____

"A grateful mind is a great mind which eventually attracts to itself great things." –Plato

This Week _____

_____

_____

_____

_____

_____

_____

_____

_____

_____

_____

Date _____

44

This Week _____

_____

_____

_____

_____

_____

_____

_____

_____

_____

Date _____

"There is no better opportunity to receive more than to be thankful for what you already have. Thanksgiving opens the windows of opportunity for ideas to flow your way." –Jim Rohn

This Week _____

_____

_____

_____

_____

_____

_____

_____

_____

_____

_____

Date _____

45

This Week _____

_____

_____

_____

_____

_____

_____

_____

_____

_____

_____

_____

Date _____

"You have no cause for anything but gratitude and joy."
–Buddha

This Week _____

_____

_____

_____

_____

_____

_____

_____

_____

_____

_____

_____

Date _____

46

This Week _____

_____

_____

_____

_____

_____

_____

_____

_____

_____

_____

Date _____

"There is a calmness to a life lived in gratitude, a quiet joy."
-Ralph Blum

This Week _____

_____

_____

_____

_____

_____

_____

_____

_____

_____

_____

Date _____

47

This Week _____

_____

_____

_____

_____

_____

_____

_____

_____

_____

_____

Date _____

"I don't have to chase extraordinary moments to find happiness-it's right in front of me if I'm paying attention and practicing gratitude." –Brené Brown

This Week _____

_____

_____

_____

_____

_____

_____

_____

_____

_____

_____

Date _____

48

This Week _____

_____

_____

_____

_____

_____

_____

_____

_____

_____

_____

_____

Date _____

"Gratitude makes sense of our past, brings peace for today, and creates a vision for tomorrow." –Melody Beattie

This Week _____

_____

_____

_____

_____

_____

_____

_____

_____

_____

_____

Date _____

49

This Week _____

_____

_____

_____

_____

_____

_____

_____

_____

_____

_____

Date _____

"When you practice gratefulness, there is a sense of respect toward others." -Dalai Lama

This Week _____

_____

_____

_____

_____

_____

_____

_____

_____

_____

_____

Date _____

50

This Week _____

_____

_____

_____

_____

_____

_____

_____

_____

_____

_____

Date _____

"Showing gratitude is one of the simplest yet most powerful things humans can do for each other." –Randy Pausch

This Week _____

_____

_____

_____

_____

_____

_____

_____

_____

_____

_____

Date _____

51

This Week _____

_____

_____

_____

_____

_____

_____

_____

_____

_____

_____

Date _____

"Gratitude is the single most important ingredient to living a successful and fulfilled life." –Jack Canfield

This Week _____

_____

_____

_____

_____

_____

_____

_____

_____

_____

Date _____

52

This Week _____

_____

_____

_____

_____

_____

_____

_____

_____

_____

_____

_____

Date _____

"Acknowledging the good that you already have in your life is the foundation for all abundance." -Eckhart Tolle

This Week _____

_____

_____

_____

_____

_____

_____

_____

_____

_____

_____

Date _____

52 Week Journal Reflections

First, decide which of you will respond as You: _____ and which of you will respond as Me: _____ for the remainder of this exercise.

How did it feel to anticipate an appreciation entry from your partner every week?

You: _____

_____

_____

_____

Me: _____

_____

_____

_____

OUR GRATITUDE JOURNAL

How did using this weekly gratitude journal enhance
your relationship with your partner?

You: _____

_____

_____

_____

Me: _____

_____

_____

_____

In what ways did this journal help to change your mindset?

You: _____

_____

_____

_____

Me: _____

_____

_____

_____

Pick your top three favorite entries that you wrote about your partner,
and explain why they are your favorites.

You:

1. _____

_____

_____

_____

2. _____

_____

_____

_____

3. _____

_____

_____

_____

Me:

1. _____

_____

_____

_____

2. _____

_____

_____

_____

3. _____

_____

_____

_____

52 Week Journal Reflections

What are your top three favorite entries that your partner wrote about you, and why?

You:

1. _____

_____

_____

_____

2. _____

_____

_____

_____

3. _____

_____

_____

_____

OUR GRATITUDE JOURNAL

Me:

1. _____

_____

_____

_____

2. _____

_____

_____

_____

3. _____

_____

_____

_____

52 Week Journal Reflections

What was the common theme you noticed that your partner appreciated most?

You: _____

_____

_____

_____

Me: _____

_____

_____

_____

How will you use what you have learned to strengthen your relationship from now on?

You: _____

_____

_____

_____

Me: _____

_____

_____

_____

Thank You

Thank you for choosing our gratitude journal! We hope the weekly gratitude journaling has enabled you and your partner to strengthen your relationship.

If you enjoyed using this journal, please leave us a review on Amazon and share it with other couples. You can even gift this book, as a wedding or anniversary gift, to your friends and family.

If you would like to receive email updates about future books, courses, and more, visit our website below to join our book fan community today.

www.ourpeacefulfamily.com/bookfan

Thank you again for choosing our journal!

Marcus and Ashley Kusi

About Marcus and Ashley

We help overwhelmed newlyweds adjust to married life, and inspire married couples to improve their marriage so they can become better husbands and wives.

We do this by using our own marriage experience, gleaning wisdom from other seasoned couples, and sharing what works for us through our website and marriage podcast, *The First Year Marriage Show.*

Visit the website below to listen to the podcast:

www.firstyearmarriage.com

Visit our website to learn more about us:

www.ourpeacefulfamily.com

Marriage is a life-long journey that thrives on love, commitment, trust, respect, communication, patience, and companionship. – Ashley and Marcus Kusi

Other Books by Marcus and Ashley

1. **Our Bucket List Adventures**: A Journal for Couples

2. **Questions for Couples**: 469 Thought-Provoking Conversation Starters for Connecting, Building Trust, and Rekindling Intimacy

3. **Communication in Marriage**: How to Communicate with Your Spouse Without Fighting

4. **Communication in Marriage**: A Companion Workbook for Couples

5. **First Year of Marriage**: The Newlywed's Guide to Building a Strong Foundation and Adjusting to Married Life.

6. **Emotional and Sexual Intimacy in Marriage**: How to Connect or Reconnect with Your Spouse, Grow Together, and Strengthen Your Marriage